OTHER BOOKS BY ROBERT M. DRAKE

Spaceship (2012)
The Great Artist (2012)
Science (2013)
Beautiful Chaos (2014)
Beautiful Chaos 2 (2014)
Black Butterfly (2015)
A Brilliant Madness (2015)
Beautiful and Damned (2016)
Broken Flowers (2016)
Gravity: A Novel (2017)
Star Theory (2017)
Chaos Theory (2017)
Light Theory (2017)
Moon Theory (2017)
Dead Pop Art (2017)
Chasing The Gloom: A Novel (2017)
Moon Matrix (2018)
Seeds of Wrath (2018)
Dawn of Mayhem (2018)
The King is Dead (2018)
What I Feel When I Don't Want To Feel (2019)
What I Say To Myself When I Need To Calm The Fuck Down (2019)
What I Say When I'm Not Saying A Damn Thing (2019)
What I Mean When I Say Miss You, Love You & Fuck You (2019)
What I Say To Myself When I Need To Walk Away, Let Go And Fucking Move On (2019)
What I Really Mean When I Say Good-bye, Don't Go And Leave Me The Fuck Alone (2019)
The Advice I Give Others But Fail To Practice My Damn Self (2019)
The Things I Feel In My Fucking Soul And The Things That Took Years To Understand (2019)

For Excerpts and Updates please follow:

Instagram.com/rmdrk
Facebook.com/rmdrk
Twitter.com/rmdrk

Book Cover: Robert M. Drake

*For The Ones Who Feel Like They've Lost
Everything*

CONTENTS

WHAT I REALLY MEAN WHEN I SAY GOOD-BYE DON'T GO AND LEAVE ME THE FUCK ALONE

ROBERT M. DRAKE

ANYMORE

It's sad.

Because

*you were once
the only person*

*I would run to
and now,*

*I barely know
who you are*

anymore.

MORE THAN ONCE

Maybe we aren't
meant for this.

Maybe we're meant
for more.

So be patient
with what hurts

and smile
at what you've learned.

The process is beautiful.

If you don't trust it.
You'll go through it

again.

And nothing
is ever lost

but time is,
if the same love

is experienced
more than once.

US AND THEM

There is you.

Me.
Us.

And then,
there is them.

And none of us
want what we deserve.

None of us want
what belongs to us.

We just want
what we crave.

Even if it hurts.

Even if it
demoralizes us.

We love
what we love

and none of us
give a damn

of what kind of pain
it brings.

Because in the end,
how it hurts

does not matter.

All that matters is,
that we loved

the way we loved

and hope
it doesn't consume us.

Hope
it doesn't completely

destroy us.

And doesn't devour
our souls

in the mist
of all the things

we owe
to ourselves.

SCARS INSIDE

You trust
without building walls.

You love
as if you've never

been hurt.

And you give
without expecting anything

in return.

You're beautiful,
baby

but this is how
you get your heart broken.

This is how
you get scars

in your heart.

HOW TO LOVE

We don't even know
why we hurt

the way we hurt.

Love
the way we love.

Want
or care

the way we do.

We just do
because we must.

Because we feel.

Because this has been
the only way

we have learned
how to heal.

How to let go.
How to cry

and laugh

and most importantly,
how to love.

GIVE IT

Some people cut
so deep

that no amount of time
could ever heal you.

No amount of love
could ever make you

forget.

It's painful.
But it's the truth.

When it's real.
It's real.

And no one could ever
take that

away from you.

No one could ever
replace

the one you give
your heart to.

SPEAK TO YOU

That sad song
is your heart.

That movie that makes you cry
is your life.

And that story
you keep

re-reading is your love.

Everything you do
reminds you

of *that* special person.

That one person
who feels the same way.

Who relates
to all the things

that speak to you.

A CLUE

You're alive
but you're not living

your life.

The same way
you want to heal

and find self-love
but you don't have

the slightest clue
where to start.

Search within.

WITH DARKNESS

It's the way you remind me
to love myself.

The way
you make me feel.

The way
you bring out

certain things about me.

Even some
I've deeply forgotten.

You make me remember
who I am

and you make me
feel soft

in a hard world.

Like a feather
falling from a skyscraper.

Like the last star
in a universe

filled with darkness.

You have saved me.
You have made me realize

how much life
I have left.

You've kept me
where I belong.

THEIR SILENCE

You have to deal
with it.

As hard as it is.

You've got to
go through it.

Deal with it,
you know?

We all
have something

that burdens us.

A scar
that we can't hide.

Something that still hurts.

But you learn
how to *deal with it*.

You learn
how to move on

from it.

And what you take
from it

solely depends on you.

The only thing
you're not allowed to do

is
run away.

Because everything
catches up to you.

Sooner or later
everything begins to hurt

all over again.

So no matter how much
it takes.

You have to face
what hurts.

You have to conquer
your fears

and demand their silence.

Respect.

Believe me,
things will hurt

a whole lot less
when you pull the knife

out of your heart

the one love
left behind.

WHAT BEGINS OR ENDS

Learning how
to love yourself

is a lifelong process.

It is not
something you can

just learn
after some tragic event.

It is not
something you just pick up

after a terrible break up.

Self-love
is an ongoing practice.

It is finding
what you love most

about yourself
in others

and spreading that same
love to those

who need it most.

It is finding
that place within you

and learning
where to find it

when you feel
a bit lost.

It is remembering
that your life

is your life
and you are enough.

Not only to those
who love you

but to yourself.

It is a journey.
One that knows no end.

And the moment
you realize this

is the moment
everything begins.

The moment
everything changes.

And the moment
you find the courage

to piece yourself
back

together again.

ACTIONS SPEAK

When it comes to you.

I just want you
to need me

the same way
I need you.

But it's the little things
that hurt me

the most.

You know,
the details.

The things you say
you'll do

but forget.

The missed calls.
The unread messages.

The way you make promises
to only break them.

I know.

Why waste my time
with you.

Why put myself through
so much anguish.

You're a good person.
That I know.

I could see
what others don't.

But still,
it's the simplest things

that suffocate me.

That shit kills me.

Some actions
speak louder than words.

And some words
are never quite enough.

Not even
for someone you love.

WHEN WE FLY

Your hands
and heart

have one thing
in common.

They can both be held
but *only one*

can break it
the moment

they let it
fall.

That's the risk we take
when we want

to be held.

USE OF WORDS

Sometimes I wonder
why your pain

clings to me.

Why the things
that hurt you,

hurt me,
although,

I know they are things
that are not currently

 happening to me.

Sometimes I wonder,
you know?

Do I love you
that much.

Do I care
that much.

To the point
where I feel

what you feel.

I'm aligned to you.
To your mind.

To your heart
and soul.

I don't know.

Maybe it's the universes way
of telling us

we're one.

Because sometimes
soulmates go through things

like this.

Or maybe
it's our way

of letting each other know
how we feel

without

the use of words.

MUCH MORE

You can't
just tell someone

to be happy.

The same way
you can't

just tell them
to move on

or to let go.

Things aren't that easy.

If you really want
to help someone,

then be there for them.

Talk to them.
Listen.

Try to put yourself
in their shoes.

No matter how much
time it takes.

And once you do,
you'll understand

how sometimes
you can't fix things

with the use of words.

*Sometimes healing
requires more.*

*So.
Much.
More.*

IN LOVE WITH YOU

*You can be wild
and you can be*

adventurous.

*As long as your heart
is free.*

*As long as you stay
true to who you are.*

*And keep your heart
madly in love*

with what you feel.

SO FUCKING GOOD ON YOU

I want you
to smile when I'm gone.

I want you
to find yourself.

To not let go
of what you believe in.

Because unlike
the other men

you've been with—the
ones you've told me about—the

ones who've broken
your heart.

I want to see you happy.

I want to see you grow
and mature and heal.

I want you
to find your peace.

To find
what makes you happy.

To chase every single thing
you told me about.

I genuinely
want these things

for you.

So when ten years
or even twenty

pass us by.

We can accidentally
run into each other somewhere,

some place,
in the middle of the world

and smile.

So that we can remember.
Remember

what it was like
to be young and full of love.

Remember
what it was like

to not have a worry

in the world
and what mattered most

so close
to our hearts.

So that we could remember
ourselves

but not in this current state
of sadness

but in all the good times
we shared.

I want us to remember each other
for the best parts we brought out

within each other.

I know,
I have more to say.

More within my heart.

But I can't find the words.
I know one day,

I will
and I know one day,
we'll see each other again.

But for now
this is good-bye.

Until then,
I'll be in the other side

of the universe,
sitting on a star,

and living my life
the way I intend to.

Don't ever forget
to smile.

It looks so fucking
good on you.

SLIP AWAY

I want to love.

But I don't want
any part of me

to hurt.

I really want to
but *only* with you.

The problem is,
I don't know where to find you.

I am here.

Waiting.
Breaking.

Wanting you
to love me

but not
let me slip away.

What an unfortunate thing
to go through.

To want to give

someone a call

but not have
a telephone to do so.

Not have
the number of the person
you love.

REMEDIES

You've been quiet
for too long.

You've held your own hand
for too long.

And you've leaned
on your own shoulder

for too long.

Isn't it time
for you

to be held by someone else?

Isn't it time for you
to be loved?

I know you're strong
but you don't have to

be alone.

You don't have to
believe

that no one

is here for you.

Trust
is a beautiful thing.

It can calm all of that rage
you have

within you.

It can give you more.

It will not just make
the flowers bloom

from your heart.

But it will also
spring water

from your soul.

It will also
stream wind

from your lungs.

And shed light
from your mind.

Let life drip

from the tip of your bones.

And let love be
the gift

that brings it all together.

The hot glue
that is never too hard

to find.

The most powerful remedy
to heal

all things that hurt.

NOT AROUND

*I don't want you
to cry over me.*

*I just want you
to remember me*

*for the way
I loved you*

*when I am
not around.*

MY NATURE

One day
you'll understand

why birds fly
the way they do.

Why the wind blows
the way it blows.

Why the wind travels
the way it travels.

And why you love
the way you love.

One day
you'll know all of these things

and understand
why you can't change

any of them.

You can't control the way
things are.

Love freely.
Openly.

And carefully.

It's in your nature
to do so.

*Every time your wounds
bleed*

they bleed love.

SAME WAY TOO

I know we spent
a lot of time together.

Years even.

But I can't seem
to remember

any of it.

I can't seem
to remember

what happened in-between.

All I could remember
is how my life was

before you.

And how my life is
after you.

The beginning
and the end.

How we met
and how we let go.

I know.

It's been a long time.
I know what it is

I must do.

Hell,
everyone around me

tells me.

But it's easier said
than done.

Easier to envision
than to do.

I know
I must move on.

And I know
when I'm around

others I put shade
to your name.

But the truth is,
I'm hurting without you.

I'm dying from the inside.

And I don't know
how to stop it.

I don't know
what to do.

Things fall apart.
Things break.

And sometimes
things never find their way

back home.

And I'm still healing.
Still learning

to be
on my own.

I've tried, baby...
I really have.

But I'm too tough
to show it.

I'm too hard
for soft hands.

And I'm sure
you feel

the same way
too.

We are strangers
looking for something we've lost.

Two humans
looking for a piece of themselves.

The flower
we always dream about

but never have
the opportunity

to hold.

THE NIGHT BEFORE

Feel me.

I love you
but you're no good
for me.

I want to stay
but I have to go.

YOUR REFLECTION

No matter what you do
or who you give yourself to.

Make sure
not to go mad.

Make sure
not to get lost

in the chaos of love.

In the chaos
of losing yourself

within another person.

Make sure
you know your way

back home.

Make sure
you don't become

one of those people
who need someone by their side

to live.

Who need to be
in a relationship to function.

Prevent this
at all cost.

Find yourself
and who you are

without losing
your goddamn soul.

Find love
without losing your heart.

Find trust
without losing your sense

of self.

And find someone
who'll walk with you.

Side by side.
Not just someone

who'll lead you
without your consideration.

Remember,
this is your life.

Your moment.

Your memory
and love.

And no one else's.

And the company
of people should be a blessing,

not a burden—a
universe full of life

and not a black hole
full of emptiness

and darkness.

Let it be known,
that you have too much

to offer
and too much

to lose
at the same time.

Too much of too much
and too little of too little.

Let it be known.

Let it *not* be forgotten.

Love freely
but carefully.

Love softly
but hard enough to protect
what you love

without losing yourself
or losing

what you are.

IN THE HEART

I want you
but I need to be alone.

I need more time.

More space.
More me

for myself.

To understand myself.

I don't want to pass
my pain to another person.

I don't want to leave
my heaviness

in the heart
of someone I love.

CONCERNS

Tell them
you love them.

Tell them
how much you need them

every time
you get the chance to.

Tell them
what you feel and think.

And don't lose it.
Don't waste it.

The future is so fucking hard
and confusing.

But don't let that stop you
from telling the people

you love
how you fccl.

Don't let it become
one of those things—something

you'll regret

when they're gone.
Love them
and act on it.

Let them know
how important they are.

It is essential to know
what you feel

and share it
with those it concerns.

SILENCE

*If you feel it
in your bones.*

*Act on it.
Go for it.*

*Don't think twice
about it.*

*One of the worst things
you can do*

*is silence
your heart.*

START NOW

Give yourself
the rest you need.

The healing you need.
Give yourself time.

We are so caught up
in the now

and in the future

and in the lives
of others that we tend

to forget
how important it is

to be alone.

Give yourself silence.

Peace.
And isolation.

It's okay to distance yourself
for a little while.

It's okay to listen

to what your soul needs.

To breathe on your own.
To do things,

even if it's nothing,
alone.

It's okay.
It really is.

There is nothing more beautiful
than a person in control

of themselves.

In control
of their feelings.

And love.
And thoughts.
And actions.

Give yourself the freedom
you need to reflect.

To break things down.

The past
and the present.

Give yourself emptiness
and put filling yourself whole

into practice.

Give yourself brokenness
and put picking up the pieces

to work.
But do it alone.

In complete isolation.

This is more a gift
than a burden.

More a blessing
than a curse.

And don't expect your solitude
to be perfect

or fully understood
because it doesn't have to be.

But expect it
to be enough.

Expect it
to be you.

Expect it
to be exactly what

you need.

That perfect balance
you're looking for.

Give yourself
the rest you need.

From time to time.

Just do it.
Start somewhere.

Start now.

YOUR ROLE

It is easy
to forget how important

your role is
to people.

Don't ever think
you do not matter.

You matter
and it is easy to forget

and ignore.

But don't.
You are important.

You matter.

Everything you do
is currently affecting

someone's life.

Including that
of your own.

SHAPE THE FUTURE

You can't go back
to how things were.

No one can.

But that doesn't mean
the good times are over.

That doesn't mean
we can't laugh

how we once did.

We can't love
and share ourselves

how we once did,

many moons ago
when we were younger.

The past
is the past

and it's a beautiful thing.

But we still have
so much

to look forward to.

So much
that we cannot even begin

to imagine it.

So much
that we can't even

predict it.

Sometimes
we have to unhook ourselves

from what we have known—from
what we are mostly

comfortable with
and welcome

the unknown.

Understand that the future
is full of hope.

The future
is a lot less toxic

than we think.
And a lot more welcoming

than we can imagine.

The future
is constantly shaped

by the past.

And the past
is constantly shaped

by the future.

And somewhere in-between
you're living the present

trying to make sense
of everything

you do.

SHALL PASS

There is something
in my bones

that keeps telling me
to keep going.

To believe in myself.

And to know,
that all things

that hurt shall pass.

I am here.
I am here.
I am here.

Trust your gut.
Trust your instincts.

Everything always
turns itself out.

Everything will be okay.

CLING TO LIFE

Cling to the things
that bring you life.

To the people
and to the love

within.

Hold on to it.
And to all of it.

It is your task
to make yourself happy.

A position
that could only be fulfilled

by you.

That could only be heard
and undone...

by you.

Your heart will save you.
It knows the way.

Therefore,

it is best
to follow it

no matter what.

It is an insult
to yourself

to do otherwise.

SADDER THAN THIS

I am not gone.

I am not broken.

Yes,
I might look different.

Sound
and think
and feel different.

I am supposed to
because I have changed.

I have gone through
hell and returned.

I've had enough
and my maturity shows it.

It blooms off the tip
of my head.

And you can tell.

And it is eating you alive.

It kills you

that I am someone else.

Someone new.

But hey,
don't feel pity toward me

because I am unrecognizable
to you.

Feel pity for yourself
because you

after all these years,
have not grown.

You
after all these years,

have stayed the same.

And there's nothing sadder
than that.

The sun rises.
The sun sets.

*And you haven't
grown at all.*

BY ACCIDENT

You can fuck me over
by accident.

You can shatter
whatever I have left,

take it with you
and let it slip away.

But for Christ's sake,
please don't lie to me.

Don't make
a fool of me

on purpose.

Don't pretend
to be someone you're not

and feed me
false hope

while I search
within myself

and give you
all that I am

and more.

In other words,
don't bullshit a bullshitter.

I've driven
through that avenue
many times before.

LIFE IS HARD

Force yourself
to bloom

when all else fails.

Force yourself
to heal.

To move on.

Life is hard
enough already.

Self-love shouldn't be
one of those things... but

if you catch yourself
dwelling on the past—living

in it.

Then find it
within yourself to do

something about it.
To move pass it.

Your heart beats,

it keeps you alive
but sometimes

you must force it
to do

a little more.

SCARS ARE MINE

Although
I have grown

and healed
and even forgotten

some of my past.

There are still some scars
that have stayed with me.

No matter what I go through
or who I meet.

There are some scars
that'll never leave me.

Some
that are meant

to remind me
of how much

it once hurt.

Of how much
I've overcome.

And of how much
more *still* I deserve.

This is my life
and some scars

are mine forever.

Sometimes
you just can't wash away

what hurts.

LIBERATE YOU

That's the thing.

You think a scar
isn't as significant

as the wound itself.
But I think you're wrong.

I believe
it's the most important part

of your healing.
Of your process.

Because it's not just
about the wound.

What caused it.
How and when.

It's about
how you heal from it.

How you treat it
and what you pick up

from the experience.

Scars,
like wounds

have their place.

And they're more
than just marks

in your soul.

They're decorations.

And the more you have,
the better you will

understand people.

Places.
Memories.

Love
and most importantly,

yourself.

They're meant
to liberate you.

Not
slow you down.

THE UPSIDE

Maybe love
is not meant to be found

in one person.

Maybe love
is a collection

of people
who've moved you.

Who've meant something
to you

in both the past
and the present.

Maybe love
is what you've learned

from experience
and from what deeply hurts.

Or maybe
it's the expectation

of what you deserve
based on

what you've been through.

Maybe love
is meant to be given away.

Meant to be lost,
to be found

all over again.

Maybe love is an ocean.
A sky full of stars.

A gentle breeze
passing us by.

And maybe
we're just a planet

full of lonely people
admiring it

from

the other side.

IN A CAGE

Maybe it's me.

Maybe I am
the one who keeps

hurting you.

The one who keeps
taking you for granted.

And maybe
I'm too blind

and too naive
to see it

any other way.

I love you
but I don't want to keep

hurting you.

I love you
but I refuse

to keep you in a cage.

TO BE OR NOT

We can still
find a way to start over.

Find a way
to build something new

together.

We can still
make it work.

It's not too late.
It never is.

If we believe it.

If we
let what we feel inside

be
what it is meant

to be.

Then we will find
each other again.

We will pick up where

we left off

And leave
all the bullshit behind.

FELT ALONE

Who would have thought?

It was going to be you
who fucked me over.

The one
who came to me

at 3 a.m.
when *you* needed me the most.

And the one
who disappeared

when I felt alone.

THE WORLD

Those random
2 a. m. texts
mean everything.

Pay attention
to the ones

who think of you
while the rest of the world

is sleeping.

YOU GET MORE

Sometimes
the only thing

you can do
is let go.

Start over.

Sometimes
it's all you're given.

You won't always have
an option.

The only choice
you have

is to live through whatever
is meant for you.

This is true
in life.

In love.
In loss.

In grief.
In healing.

Sometimes
you don't get

what you deserve.

Sometimes,
in the end,

you get more.

WHAT YOU THINK

Take a deep breath.

Fill your lungs
with the stardust

all around you.

You're a lot tougher
than you know.

A lot stronger.
And you still

have a fight in you.

Don't let what burdens you
weigh you down.

You're made of both
chaos and order.

And them
leaving you

shouldn't break you.

It should make you.
You're existence

is a goddamn miracle.

You're life
is a whole lot

more valuable
than you think.

THE THING

That's the thing
about losing someone.

You never quite
get over them.

You never quite
stop missing them.

You never quite
stop wondering,

if maybe one day,
they'll walk through your door

and greet you
with a smile.

Sometimes grief
can last a lifetime.

And

sometimes a lifetime
feels a lot longer

than we think.

YOUR PROCESS

Some people
only accept you

for who
you once were.

For what you said
and did...

disregarding
who you are now.

Disregarding,
if you've grown up

or changed.

Some people
only hang on

to the old you.

They take the future
for granted

and miss your process
completely.

A BEAUTIFUL THING

Accept who you are.
What you feel.

What you love
and don't love.

Accept your face.

Your thoughts
and heart.

Feel your soul.
Do all things with soul.

No matter what you
think of it.

Accept it.
All of it.

It's who you are.

Now take a deep breath
and let it all go.

*Being free
is a beautiful thing.*

TOO HARD

You've worked too hard
on yourself

to give up now.

And you've gone through
so much shit

to just
sit back and cry.

To just
do nothing

and wilt all day.

Yes,
the storm is hard.

Yes,
the ground and your world

do sometimes shake
but it is never

off course.

It keeps going.

It keeps moving forward
and it doesn't stop

for no one
and neither should you.

DEFINES YOU

There's a little bit
of magic *everywhere.*

There's even some
in you.

ALWAYS WITH LOVE

If you're serious
about love

then you have to
find it within.

You have to give yourself
permission to heal.

To move on.

I know it might sound cliché
but you really have to

let things go.

You really have to
grow up sometime

and accept
all the things

you deserve.

All the things
you see yourself getting into.

Some good.

Some bad.

If you're serious
about finding love.

Just remember.

Love.
Always.

Starts within.

I hope you never
forget that.

I hope you genuinely
learn how to love yourself.

CARE OF YOU

It is exhausting,
I know.

Telling them how you feel.

Showing them
how much you love them.

And making them
a priority

above anything else.

It's terribly exhausting,
I know.

Taking care of someone else,
when no one

is taking care
of you.

FEEL GOOD

That's the thing,
it's hard

to not fall in love
with someone

you spend
a lot of time with.

It's hard
for the heart

to ignore
the few people

who make you feel good
about yourself.

Even if it lasts
for a few moments.

Even if it's too good
to be true.

We fall in love
with whom

we fall in love with.

And we never ask questions
or try to stop it.

It sort of just happens
on its own.

LOVE HARD

Love hard.

*And when you feel
as if*

*you've had enough.
Love harder.*

IF YOU...

If you let it happen,
it will keep happening.

You will keep hurting.
You will keep suffocating.

You have to learn
when to say

enough.
Learn how to say it.

How to move forward with it.
Because enough,

is enough.

You're too much
of a good person to go through hell.

Especially,
all alone.

You're soul is too beautiful
to be in agony all the time.

And your heart
is too precious

to be aching.

To be barely living.

You have to learn,
my sweet love.

You have to know
when to let go.

When to move forward.
When to do things

for yourself
and only yourself.

I cannot do these things
for you.

I cannot make you see
what you deserve.

Make you go for it,
take risks, you know?

I cannot.

But I can
be there with you.

I can

stand beside you,
to make sure

you don't completely shatter.
To make sure

you don't completely
hit the ground

and never find
your way back up.

I cannot make you change
and I can't stop things

from happening.

Only you
can do that

but I can surely,
be there with you.

You no longer have to
cry on your own.

You no longer
have to pick yourself up

all alone.

I am here.

And I always will be.

A best friend
should always be close by.

And I will always be here
especially

in your darkest times.

STAY AWAY

Stay away
from anyone

who doesn't look back
when you say

good-bye.

WHEN THEY LEAVE

We are here to love
and cry.

To break and heal.

To share our loneliness
with others

and to search
for those who understand

what it's like
to pick up the pieces

when the people
we love

leave.

THE BEGINNING

Self-love is what happens
when you revisit

what once hurt.

And realize,
how the pain

never existed.

It was all
in your head

from the very start.

SECOND CHANCE

There is still
a chance for you

to love.

There is still
a lot of time left.

Never stop believing in it.
You will find it.

One day,
you will see,

how everything you thought
you lost

never left you.

How everything you thought
you found

has always been
within you

from the start.

ART

Because pain
turns to art.

And sometimes
what hurts

is far more beautiful
than you think.

THEY CARE

Maybe he does love you,
who knows.

But words are words
and actions are actions.

And I've witnessed
enough brokenness throughout

the years to know
the difference.

And with all heart
I can tell you this.

Maybe he does care.
Maybe he does love you.

Maybe you are
his favorite.

So he says.
But how many times

has he made you feel alone.

How many times
has he filled your heart

with anger
and sorrow.

How many times
have you felt the bitterness.

The emptiness.
The endless void

that leads to nowhere.

How many times
have you cried...

enough tears
to fill an entire ocean.

Ask yourself.
How many?

And if your answer is
too many... then

by all means
that alone speaks volumes.

That alone
should be the answer

you're looking for.

Yes.
Maybe he does

"love you"

but you my dear,
deserve a lot more.

You my dear,
deserve to do

what makes you happy
but also, to do it

with the right people.

With ones
who show you they care.

Keep shining sad girl.
You are, indeed,

everything
plus a little more.

BEAUTIFUL

Maybe all of the pain
you've endured

isn't your fault.

Maybe none of it
was actually caused

by you.

But when it is all
said and done.

You must take
the proper steps to heal.

To move on.
To let go.

To outgrow whatever
it was that caused you suffering.

It is your responsibility
to make the best

of all outcomes.

And it is an essential part

of becoming
who you are.

The process
is undeniably beautiful.

Trust it.
ALWAYS.

YOU WILL SEE

One day
you are going to realize

how important self-care
and self-love are.

And when that day comes,
you will sincerely apologize

to yourself
for all the times

you wasted on the people
who made you feel

unwanted.
Who made you feel

hard to love
and even more confused

about what you're thinking
and feeling.

One day,
you will be forced to rebuild.

Forced to grow.

Forced to stop grieving
over your past

and walk away
from the ghost

who can't seem to leave.

One day,
you will realize this…

how sometimes
the most beautiful people

rise from the fire
and bloom softly

from the hardest roads.

One day
you'll see.

One day
it'll all make sense.

TO REVEAL

We all need
at least one person

to run to.

One person
to listen to what hurts.

Who could keep
all your secrets

no matter how much
of yourself

you choose to reveal.

NEVER EASY

Growing up is never easy.

And now looking back
I wish I had someone

to tell me
the things I now know.

The things that took years
and years to learn.

If you're still an adolescent.
Then I will tell you

what I needed to hear
when I was your age

in hopes
that maybe it will help you

see things
for what they are.

I will tell you that fear
is all in your head.

That you create it
based on your doubt.

Based on how you see yourself
and the worry of being rejected.

I will tell you
that you don't need to be

accepted by anyone
but yourself.

That acceptance is another word
for following the crowd.

For not thinking for yourself.
(in most cases)

I will tell you
to look at yourself in the mirror.

To know you are important.
To know that you have purpose.

That your voice
really does matter.

I will tell you to be good to people.
To be good to those

you don't know.

To those who need more love.
To those who have been rejected.

To stand up for them.
Fight for them.

I will tell you
that everything changes.

That nothing ever lasts long enough.
To enjoy your time

as things run their course.

To take all moments in
with your soul.

To learn as much as you can.
To share what you love

with those you love.

And to be kind to yourself
when you need it most.

I will tell you
to not take yourself

so goddamn serious
all the time.

That there is a time
and place for both good

and bad things.

That you must experience both
at the cost of growing up.

There are too many things
I wish someone could have told me.

Too many to write.

The bottom line is,
to live your life.

To not let anyone dictate it.
To be yourself.

To heal at your own pace.
To not compare yourself

to anyone
and to move on

when you must
and hold on

when you know
there is something worth fighting for.

Growing up is never easy.
And it shouldn't be.

Just remember,
the harder your journey is.

The bigger
your heart will be.

HOPE

*You can't lose hope
on people.*

*Everybody has
a little love in them*

somewhere.

YOUR PAST

Don't expect me
to be perfect.

Expect me
to be honest.

Expect me
to be enough.

And don't expect me
to give you the same kind

of love
you received

by someone
in your past.

DOUBT IT

Self-doubt is a motherfucker
and what you dislike

about yourself
should never be ignored

or disregarded.

No.

Give them time.
Work on the things

you don't like
about yourself.

Those are the parts of you
that need the most attention.

That need
the most love.

FEEL MORE

We are lovers.

You and I.
We don't know

how to let go.

And we don't understand
how sometimes

loving someone can cause
more harm to us

than good.

But that's the problem
and that will *ALWAYS BE*

the problem.

Our hearts blind us.
And we follow

what we feel
more than we should.

A MILLION THINGS

And then
she asked me why

I didn't love her.

She asked why
I loved the other one—the
other woman.

And I tried very hard
to resist.

I tried very hard
to swallow the truth.

To bury it
deep within my bones.

And then,
in a blink of an eye,

I spewed.

I couldn't resist the truth.

It fell out of me
like a river following its course.

Like a bottle
erupting.

Spilling empty.
Till there was nothing left.

At least
not for me.

*"She makes me feel
like a different person.*

*Living
in a different planet.*

*Feeling
a million different things.*

All at once."

And that was all
I had to say

about that.

OF THE WORLD

There are ways
of letting them know

how you feel
without the use of language.

Without the use of words.

Silence
is the sound you hear

when you've heard enough.
It is sharp enough

to shatter your soul
but also,

loud enough
to hear

from the other side
of the world.

GIVE IT BACK

It's hard to write
when you have an audience.

It's hard to be true
to yourself as an artist.

Things were simpler
way before the fame.

Things were easier
to get off my chest.

And now,
I have to watch

what I write.

What I say
and feel

and do.

I can't be myself anymore
because something

is *always* bound to offend someone.
Somewhere.

It hurts to say.
But I don't know

who I am anymore.

I can't even remember
who I was.

They have taken my soul.
And they have yet,

to give it back.

I belong to the people.
I belong in their hearts.

Leave me there.
Find me there.

Love me there.

SHARE IT

It's simple.

The harder you love.
The harder you care.

And the harder you give.

The harder it'll hurt
in the end.

But you should never
let that stop you.

Keep going.

Never stop believing.
Never stop sharing

who you are.

FACE IT NOW

You can't just move
and think

everything will
erase itself—fix itself.

You can't run away
from what hurts.

Eventually,
your demons will find you.

And they will taunt you.
They will try to drown you

and suck the life
from your lungs.

And you won't be able
to do anything about it.

Not unless
you face them alone.

Destroy the doubt.
Defeat what hurts.

Rise and grow

one day at a time.

Because most people believe
that moving to a new environment

will force change.
Will force a new beginning.

But that's not
how it works.

Fix yourself from within.
Save yourself from within.

Because it always starts
from within.

Day in and day out.

Chaos is born from the heart
but also, dies in the heart.

No matter who you are with.
Or where you decide to go.

Face it.
Don't let it define you.

HOME OUT OF YOU

At some point.

You have to realize
if they don't love you

then no amount of love
you give them

is going to change that.

No amount of tenderness
or care.

If they don't love you
they *just don't* love you.

It's as simple as that.
And it's important to realize this

you should never
make a home

of those who are not willing
to make a home

out of you

PERIOD.

YOU LOVE

My dear,

instead of looking for love-

the one you think
someone *will* give you.

Why don't you search
for it from within.

Self-love
is the best kind of love.

It is one you create for yourself.
To later share it

with someone you love.

A FRIEND OF MINE

A friend of mine sends me a message.

She says,
her best friend's father just died.

That it was tragic
and that she doesn't know

how to fulfill
or how to comfort her friend.

She tells me she needs some good words.
So she came to me

because I've been through it before.

I sit back and think.

And think.
And think.

After all,
I have taken it to be
my responsibility to write back.

She is a darling to me.

I inhale and remember my brother's face.
My brother's life and say,

"I think death is normal.
It's going to happen to all of us.

But I think
once you realize it's just

another phase. Another process,
then it doesn't bother you as much.

We all die.

That's a fact that is hard
to swallow but once you do.

You see how special it is
to appreciate life for what it is.

How special it is
to appreciate who you still have

now. Living. You know?

Death is harsh
but it definitely isn't the end.
Only the beginning."

She tells me thank you.

And I tell her I haven't even begun to say
what I was going to start. That was only my
opener.

She says she's heard enough.
And that those simple words

gave her the courage
she needed

to help her
bring her friend

some peace.

Sometimes you say and do something
without realizing it.

Sometimes that is all that is needed.

The beginning of something.
The end of something

you have yet to know.

MAGIC

There's magic
in conversation.

Sometimes staying up late
with someone you love

is a remedy
to all things

that worry the heart.

Sometimes a little time.
And a little love.

Is enough.

Don't be afraid to open up.
Sometimes it's all you need.

Sometimes a good friend
is enough

to save a life.

"THE SCIENCE OF…" SERIES
IS COMING SOON - SPRING OF 2020